All individual contributions © original authors.
Introduction and editorial material © Gary Carr 2025
This volume © Burton Runaway Writers 2025

This work may not be reproduced in whole or in part without express permission of the copyright holders.

All Rights Reserved

First Published March 2025 by Runaway Writers.

ISBN 978-1-0684228-0-5

Entanglement

Contents

Introduction	1
Dedication	1
Lost Property	2
Death & Morphine	6
Brother Geraldine Sister Lucifer	7
A Trickery of Tears	8
Off-screen Disaster	11
Hawk	12
An A to Z of Water	13
Timeslip	14
On Looking at a Buddleia	16
Growing Together	17
The Abduction of Grandad	18
Speed Date with a Coach my Age	21
Not Here	22
Escaping	23
Goodbyes and Hellos	24
Balancing Act	26
Shaking Off the Blackness	27
SLR	28
Seasons' Entanglement	29
Word of the Day – Entanglement	30
The Fisherman and the Moon	31
The Jasmine Girl and the Fisher's Dream	32

Introduction

Runaway Writers was formed in 2004 by four writers who found themselves without a group in Burton-on-Trent.

In the 20+ years since the group formed numbers have waxed and waned, most of the membership has changed and – since Covid – we have found ourselves with both online and face-to-face meetings every month.

The re-introduction of live meetings in 2024 brought several new members to the group and we thought that the production of the group's second anthology *Entanglement* would provide a focus for the group to work together on.

Entanglement represents the current state of our group and its writing. As a generalist writing group we have poetry and prose writers, some just starting out, others well-published. In this book, as in our meetings, everyone's contributions add to the richness of the experience.

The group can be contacted by email on:
runaway.writers.bot@gmail.com

Dedication

This anthology is dedicated to the memory of Mal Dewhirst, poet and playwright, who inspired the group for more than 15 years both with his enthusiasm and his practical abilities. Two of his pieces, written for group activities, bookend this anthology with the permission of his partner, Ann Cook.

Lost Property

Mal Dewhirst

George and Jane Johnson enter the lost property office, where they encounter the lost property attendant Eric.

ERIC
  Good morning, Sir, Madam.
GEORGE
  Ah yes, good morning. Is this the lost property office?
ERIC
  Well, that depends on your perspective.
JANE
  What do you mean, 'perspective'?
ERIC
  Well from your point of view it may be the lost property office.
  (BEAT. FROWNS) I presume you have lost something?

George nods.

ERIC
  (SMILES) But from my point of view it is the found property office. I have hundreds of items that have been found; it is only the owners that are unknown.
JANE
  So from your point of view it's the owners who are lost?
ERIC
  Except that I never knew the owners, so I could not lose them. They are not lost to me. My only link to them is that I have a found item.
GEORGE
  Well if you say so. So, can you help me? I.....
ERIC
  First things first. I need your details, we are computerised now. (BEAT) So you are....?
GEORGE
  George Johnson. And this is my wife Jane.

Eric taps into a computer.

ERIC
>Date of birth?

GEORGE
>25th August 1952.

>*Eric taps this into the computer.*

ERIC
>Right, here we are. George Johnson, and a list of everything you have ever lost. (BEAT) My, my, we have been careless over the years.

JANE
>What on earth do you mean?

ERIC
>Well, in 1957, George lost his father's car keys on the beach at Bournemouth. They were never found.

GEORGE
>I did! How amazing something like that's on a computer.

ERIC
>Then, in 1962, you lost your two front teeth in a fight with one Gruffer Smedley.

JANE
>I didn't know you got into fights, George.

GEORGE
>Just kids' stuff.

ERIC
>Hardly kids' stuff, you said his parents weren't married; called him a 'right little bastard'.

>*George looks startled.*

ERIC
>Oh dear! You were unlucky in 1965; you lost your grandfather's glass eye. I might have it here, I have hundreds of them.

GEORGE
>Yes, well, about...

ERIC
>What else do we have? Ah, yes, your virginity. I don't know why we record that because strictly speaking you can't lose your virginity. Once it's gone, you can't reclaim it as such. No, really you give it away on a non-returnable basis.

GEORGE
    I say...

ERIC
    Yes, it's all here. You lost your virginity on March 12th 1969 in the back of a red mini in Hounslow, to one Mary Smith.

JANE
    George!!

GEORGE
    I don't remember that.

ERIC
    Yes, it says you have a tendency to lose your memory when it suits you. It says you did on many occasions between 1972 and 1983 when you lost various amounts of money on horses.

JANE
    You said you'd been mugged!

GEORGE
    I was (BEAT) several times.

ERIC
    Then there is the lost weekend in 1986. It seems Mary Smith was involved in that event, also.

JANE
    You said it was pressure of work; you needed some space; some time alone; not a rekindling of your lost youth with some tart in the back of a mini.

ERIC
    It wasn't the back of a mini this time but a hotel in Eastbourne.

GEORGE
    It wasn't like that!

ERIC
    She lost an earring in the sheets. We have it here. If you want, I could let you have it to return to her.

JANE
    GEORGE!

GEORGE
    Now, Jane, it's not what you think! He's making it up. These things never happened.

JANE
    Never happened? You admitted losing your Father's car keys and your two front teeth, but the rest is made up, is it?

George turns to Eric.

GEORGE
Now listen, you. I don't know what you're trying to do here, but you need to make it clear that this is nonsense; that you've made it all up.

ERIC
Me? Sir, I am just trying to show you how good the technology is these days. I suspect you came in here to reclaim the umbrella you left on the number 21 bus to Hounslow.

JANE
Hounslow! You said you lost it on the Northern Line! You said nothing about Hounslow.

Eric produces an umbrella.

JANE
Give that to me!

Jane snatches the umbrella from Eric, George and Jane leave, Jane hitting George with the umbrella, Jane ranting.

ERIC
I think we'll leave this record open. I wouldn't be surprised if George loses one or two other things fairly soon. People really should be more careful.

Death & Morphine

Sarah Ann McCay

In the darkest corner
Of the bazaar
The local men sit
Around the shisha
Mixing wisdom with opiates.

Spices and fruits
Fragrantly share
Their scents with
Sweet smoke;
Twisting and turning,
Taking tangled words into the night,
Careless on its journey.

In the darkest corner
A dark figure
Sits and watches
The men as they smoke.
Who will go first?

Brother Geraldine Sister Lucifer

John Carpenter

"Brother Geraldine," says Lucifer
Stark upright on all fours,
"I do believe we've never met
ten hundred times or more."

"My dearest Sister Lucifer,"
replies sweet Geraldine,
"I've seen your face in every place
that I have never been!"

I will not contradict this pair,
though both are telling lies,
for crossing realms transpersonal
I travel in disguise.

And of those realms transpersonal,
where mysteries unfold,
I know more than I think I know
at least that's what I'm told

The devil's in the detail though,
whatever that may mean
thus Lucifer's fedora
is worn by Geraldine

And Geraldine's sarcophagus
is Lucifer's man cave
(her animus spreads everywhere
like tree roots in his grave)

Eventually they'll break their crowns
whilst doing dodgy capers;
you'll read about it soon enough
in all the Sunday papers.

And so hello goodbye ciao-ciao
for now that's all I'm sharing
just keep your pencil sharp my friends
and write what's right with daring.

A Trickery of Tears

Alison Sleigh

Over 100 bodies found in disappearance case

Forensic anthropologists from around the world have been called to identify thousands of bones dredged from a recently discovered lake. Mystery surrounds the grisly discovery but it appears to be linked to the recent disappearance of Miss Maureen Micklehurst.

Between the time of dinosaurs and man, giants roamed the earth. They reached for things beyond their enormity and gave their prayers to the king and queen of the heavens. The queen, they realised, controlled the vast oceans and they wandered with the tides searching for the greeting point between moon and waters, while the king shunned his wife, driving her into the darkness. The werifesteria* of giants often led to melancholy so despite nature's beauty surrounding them their numbers dwindled until only one remained.

Lonnie, with her matted mane of green hair and hands as large as magnolia trees, rested on top of the craggy hillside beneath her lunar god's glow. Her head lay on the patchy earth, hair trailing down the rock face while her body curled foetally around the lengthening hole she was lazily picking with her finger.

Queen Moon whispered, "What is the matter my child?"

"What's my purpose? I wander this land meandering with the waterways, chasing the ebb and flow of salty life but as these two friends meet and celebrate with foamy jubilation I envy their union, for mine will never come."

With this, huge tears rolled over her cheeks plopping noisily into the opening that was forming under her scratching nails.

Without friends or partners I am but an empty shell," she sighed.

Lonnie continued to scrape fervently now until she could squeeze her hand into the gap and shovel loamy waste aside creating a crater as deep as her despair.

Her tears continued streaming with pace now, filling the void taking only a fraction of her pain with them.

Kindly the queen smiled, "Jut look at the glory of your purpose. The immensity of your feelings has given you the power to create beauty that will transcend eras. Now rest. Rest for eternity my beautiful moon-child for you have found your purpose. Your purpose is to live, experience and die."

Lonnie's tears strained through solidifying mineral as the rock welcomed her home. Her green curls descended across the landscape sprouting and blooming with boughs of yew and ash. Eventually her entirety sighed and settled as she shed her remaining despair into the lake below.

Now Lonnie's Loch is hidden by the growth of a million years. Those who dare to seek her lake of tears will find their own purpose as Lonnie welcomes despair and thrives upon it. She will greedily take it from you and transform it into something beautiful.

This was the fable Mo had heard from her mother so many times it had felt like a prophecy. While her mother lay bed-ridden, barely recognising her only daughter and with no recollection of the fable Mo knew it was time to seek the change she desperately needed. Mo's dreams had mapped her journey the night her mother breathed her last but it would be three months before her courage was stronger than her grief. With a cooler and vials, and a plan to sell the magical fluid when she found it, Mo set off to deliver her despair and exchange it for a chance to thrive again.

On Tuesday 18th January the red Fiat Panda belonging to Miss Maureen Micklehurst was discovered along the R200 turn-off named locally as Moon's Descent due to the trail's drop off into the bay directly in-line with the Moon's orbital path.

Where the road leads to the footpath into the forest beyond, a coolbox was recovered containing 20 vials of an unlabelled substance. Chemical analysis revealed this to be a mescaline-based derivative which has hallucinogenic properties. It is believed that Miss Micklehurst had been exposed to the deadly concoction. Her whereabouts are currently unknown, however drone footage had exposed the position of a previously undiscovered lake.

Despite its idyllic appearance the area has been cordoned off by UK Health Security Agency (UKHS) after fears that the water was the source of the deadly substance found in the vials. From the bottom of the lake human remains were found and are still being forensically investigated.

*Werifesteria - Old English, to wander lovingly through the woods in search of mystery

Off-screen Disaster

Marjorie Neilson

I've never been to LA
seen the palm trees.
Envied the million-dollar mansions
behind gated fences.
Glamour hiding from small town America
with its checkout girls and their wannabe dreams
bought in discount stores.

I've never seen those big white letters
Hollywood emblazoned on hillside
or been some B-list tourist with a map, driving
past cafes, malls and diners
wondering if the woman in the black dress
is a someone I should recognize.

But I have seen on my TV screen
the landscape of metal – a Spielberg
disaster movie set – orange flames, acrid smoke
engulfing homes. Fame and gold statues dying
in tangled, twisted, growling metal.

I've watched the rich and famous.
The poor and middle class wander
between rows of hand-me-down clothes
piled like garbage on desert soil.
Oscar de Larenta glamour, rejected
for Primark's or Walmart's naked comfort.

I've watched as pink retardant bombs land.
Redwood trees, limos, animals once manicured gardens,
all water-bombed by helicopters and planes
from dawn until the coming of a night sky;
the coldness of moon and stars,
decried by unhelpful political rhetoric.

Continued…

Hawk

David Walton

Alarmed, nothing stirred,
faster than its shadow
burnt umber pinions blurred
skimmed the lawn low.

Veered up violently, unchecked velocity,
through tangled twists of bark
out and wheeled about, unstinting rapidity
spiralling in again through the dark.

And out to rest, on its watching tower,
sickles fiercely fastened to fence rail.
Arrogant and poised, in the stillness of the hour,
the decapitator, in luteous legs and grey fan tail.

From my porchway
I just had time to say-

Quick! Look below
before it rampaged away
along the hedge way
faster than its shadow.

An A to Z of Water

Richard Bell

Aqueducted,
Bucket filler,
Cress before,
Dribbling divinely.
Effervescent.
Fishy
Gutter gurgler.
H_2O
Island lapper
Jettied
Kingfishered.
Lolly (ice),
Miller's mate,
Newt haven.
Ocean maker
Puddle jumpee
Quagmirer
Riparian rippler.
Scalder, soother
Toe tested.
Ullswater.
Very
Wet.
Xebec sailway.
Your body (65%)
Zambezi, Zambezi.

Timeslip

David Walton

She was just a table away. The man tried not to let her catch him looking and was reminded of Cartier-Bresson positioning a camera on a cafe table to snap shots of unposed people while the photographer looked away.

The man sat outside in the shade where he could watch the crowds but not too close to the smell of traffic and the waiter seemed in no hurry to take his order. The sun was out but heavy showers had been forecast. The yellow plastic chairs not too uncomfortable and, from experience, the food adequate. When, finally, the waiter came, the man ordered Turkish coffee and a small glass of Courvoisier.

The man watched her every delicate, unaffected gesture. She still wore no jewellery, her refined ring-less finger playing with a length of hair. Her nails clean, unpainted. She took out a discreet compact mirror, not out of vanity but to look for a speck caught in her eye. The sun caught the glass and for a second the reflected ribbon of light crossed his face.

Then her friends arrived, three girls, four boys, tables were pushed together and, purposely, she sat next to his table, diagonally opposite. The good looking and well-groomed youths, he judged to be in their early twenties, they appeared relaxed in the company of the girls, and she did not seem particularly interested in them. Two girls shared knowing glances. They all drank water, no one ordered wine, no one smoked, the conversation muted, measured.

Perhaps they were at the university, or from an office, planners, or architects? The man remembered how she had shown an aptitude for drawing. Were her parents still alive? They had been so very frail. So many questions.

She was not beautiful, not in a classical sense, nor glamorous, nor, God forbid, sexy. What he loved about her was her grace, her gentle ways and most of all the inclination of her smile.

She had ordered paella and when the waiter brought it, she clearly had not expected such a piled high large dish. Amused, the man watched as she ate frugally, eating little of the saffron rice but enjoying the prawns. She dabbed her lips with a napkin.

Tread softly. He had to look away.

She wore an elegant short sleeve, lightly patterned top that suited her. In the design there was a hint of green, her favourite colour. She never glanced his way although she knew he sat there. She did not intend cruelty, but he felt her indifference.

They were young when first they met, going steady by the time they left school, then, somehow, he had lost his way. She left him. He took it badly. Tried to end it all.

As she talked unaffectedly to the waiter clearing plates, the man watched her through the reflection of the plate glass window. In the dark reversal of the glass, he saw himself, the other, an outsider, hardly recognisable, a different being, and for a moment she too gazed absent-mindedly into the blackness and in that brief illusion their images merged.

She wiped a splash of rainwater, like morning dew from her forehead, and the man was reminded of how she had regarded her hairline too high, but for him, the healthy glow of her young fresh complexion made him want to reach out. Touch her cheek. Tell her how much he missed her. Spin words. Be her Cyrano de Bergerac.

The rain came. A sudden violent downpour, water cascaded off the edge of the awning. A scraping of chairs as customers hurried undercover. "The sun is out, the sky is blue." At sixteen, in those unworldly days she had been shy, demure. Now in her twenties, she was assured, eloquent, poised, complete.

An elderly passer-by, dripping, took refuge, steadied himself, gripping a pole next to the man's table. He studied the passer-by's hand, the parchment-like skin, the green rope-like veins, the traces of arthritis, the way the fleshy liver-spotted skin took on the ridged appearance of desiccated, crumpled tissue paper.

Much like his own.

On Looking at a Buddleia

Jayne Stanton

A buddleia in early spring needs pruning.
March is recommended.
It's now April.

Monty has long since
pruned his buddleia. It's time
to don that gardening gear.

A buddleia in need
of a hard prune
is hard work.

A buddleia, and a gardener
wielding loppers and pruning saw:
food for the shredder.

If pruning a buddleia takes some time,
how much longer does it take
to dispose of the body parts?

One needs to stand back
in order to appraise
the bloody buddleia.

Knowing *how* hard
to prune – *that* is the gift
of hindsight.

Growing Together

Sarah Dale

When we first met, so long ago, I'd fallen at his feet by pure chance; grass green, just a slip of a girl, reed slender. He was so young and strong, so beautifully made, smooth and firm – what could I do but look up to him?

And he was kind to me, sheltered me from bitter winds that could have snapped me like a dry twig, funnelled the rain down his sleek sides to my roots. And of course, I grew, as is the nature of my kind, but while I grew, he, as is the nature of his kind, did not.

So while we are both rooted, fixed by our natures to the place where we are set, he, lacking my power of growth, has aged, aged terribly, so his youth's beauty and strength have become wistful memories. Now I keep him standing; hold him with my strong arms, secure his shifting foundations with my interlacing roots.

His once clear voice is cracked like an old man's, he is bent out of shape, and an ignorant person might call him ugly. My smooth green leaves stroke his scarred skin – we whisper together, our voices soft, rustling. Who are you to judge what we may have to say to each other?

My living heart wood holds his dreams – even when he is fallen as low, as dumb as the broken bones of those long dead men who raised him, seeds of mine will sing the love songs he sang me.

The Abduction of Grandad

Richard Bell

The scribbled note squeezed on the back of a cigarette packet appeared to have been written by a very shaky hand. It read, "Our Anne bring money to the Coop and they will let me go." The note was unsigned.

I had joined Phil at Baz's house where we had agreed to meet before going into town. Grubber said he would meet us later as he had to attend to some important business first. Rhubarb Ron, a friend of Baz's father, was also there – armed with a fearsome looking garden fork claiming that he and Baz's father were going to do a spot of rough digging on the allotment. Baz's father disappeared saying he had to call for something on the way and would meet Ron there. "Fab," said Ron, which we had worked out a while back was code for the Four Ale Bar at the pub opposite the allotment

Baz's mother, Anne, was clearly very worried,." It looks like my father's writing, but what can it mean? I hope nothing has happened to him". Rosalind, Baz's sister did her best to reassure her mother that it couldn't be anything serious.

"Well, you never know your luck." Rhubarb Ron's interruption didn't really help. It looked as if he was about to say more, but a withering look from Rosalind, what Baz called "the paint stripper", plus the suggestion that Ron should do something which didn't appear to be physically possible, stopped him in his tracks.

Phil, who always had a cool head, did his best to calm things down although I am not sure that it was helpful to use words like "Ransom Note"," Kidnap" and "Abduction" and to wonder whether one or two red smears on the note were blood stains.

Grandad and Ron were always a bit "up and down" with each other, particularly when Grandad claimed, as he often did, that he had been a "Desert Rat" serving under General Montgomery in the Western Desert during the Second World War and that he was on first name terms with "Monty.".

According to Ron, the nearest Grandad had ever been to a desert was the beach at Blackpool and he was more likely to have fought in the Boer War "And I mean," he would add, "spelt B O R E"

Grubber arrived at this point hot foot from the Coop where he had called to buy the ingredients for his latest culinary creation, beetroot and prune trifle, which he had tried out on us the week previously. Clearly our verdict that it was a "Moving experience of the wrong sort," or, as Phil put it, "An enema too far," had not discouraged him from attempting to bring his latest masterpiece into the world. In his defence, Grubber claimed that in the pursuit of culinary excellence, which was his mission, "You have to push the boundaries."

There was, according to Grubber "A right commotion going on at the Coop." Phil wanted to know if there was a police presence and when Grubber said there was, Baz's mother grabbed her coat and headed for the door instructing us all to follow her to the Coop immediately as Grandad was in grave danger.

When we got to the Coop, in fact well before we got to the Coop, we discovered that there was indeed "A right commotion going on," and that at the centre of it all was Grandad. All we could see at first were Grandad's legs sticking up in the air. When we got a little nearer we could see that he seemed to have nosedived into a shopping trolley to which he was chained and in which he was now firmly wedged. He was making a lot of noise. In the end with the help of a pair of bolt cutters and the application of Rhubarb Ron's fork to Grandad's bottom we managed to prise Grandad from the shopping trolley.

Baz's mother handed Grandad's captors a pound for his release although it seemed that they might be prepared to release him for nothing or might even be prepared to hand over a bit of cash if we would take him off their hands. Rhubarb Ron was of the view that a bag of washers would have been more than enough but made sure that he was some distance from Anne and Rosalind when he spoke.

A limping and loudly complaining Grandad was escorted home, where he was placed on a large cushion and interrogated.

According to Grandad he had gone to the Coop to buy some cigarettes when he saw that a crowd had gathered around a group of girls. "Lovely girls they were, just like our Rosalind," he said.

After pausing to allow further questioning, mainly from Rosalind, it emerged that the girls were students raising money for charity by asking for volunteers to be chained to a shopping trolley, who would then be released in exchange for a small charitable donation.

"Well, I thought it were a good idea, and they were lovely girls, so I volunteered. Then they said if anybody in the crowd coughed up a couple of quid they would let me go but nobody stumped up not even when they knocked it down to a pound, so that's when I wrote the note to our Anne."

Grandad was rather vague on the subject of how he had managed to become wedged in the trolley, but it seemed to be something to do with dropping the "fag packet" in the trolley, bending over the trolley to recover the note, falling in headfirst and being "Stuck there like a load of shopping." Added to this he had somehow managed to cut his finger in the process.

"And another thing," continued Grandad, "I don't think it were necessary for Ron to prod my backside with that fork, him saying it were only way to lever me out. I'll not be able to wear these trousers again. Hardly worn in they are, only had 'em for twenty-seven years"

"Well," said Anne, "All I can say is thank goodness you were wearing commodious underwear with all those people about."

Grandad was silent for a moment, then:
"Aye, it's a good job I were wearing long johns. Still got 'em from when I were in desert. It were right cold at night out there. The lads had a saying, 'Keep your long johns handy, but dunna get 'em sandy'. Mark my words, if you didn't give 'em a good shake before you put 'em on the sand played havoc with your…"

Rosalind's hand placed firmly cross Grandad's mouth prevented him from completing the sentence.

Speed Date with a Coach my Age

Gary Carr

I find it odd that we should never meet,
having travelled in so many ways such oddly similar streets,
our lives so parallel so long. Odd I suppose to me, not you –
being a coach, and all, I don't see
too much introspection being what you do.

Both conceived in nineteen-sixty, born in sixty-one;
those could-do-better school-run years done
by seventy-nine, and I think I'm fine
with you not liking punk, a line
of safety pins along a coach
or tartan livery might encroach
on customer confidence, but even mine
were never genuine;
nor my plastic, rockers' "leather" jacket,
but my eighties curls were real, cost…
well, you know…
an Enfield plasterer's pay packet.

And from the eighties, through to now, that stress
brought on by office years, your progress
was halted, mine… well… progressed
I must confess the Belgians broke
you down a little more than me. My folk
in Brussels possibly less rude,
less damaging than yours in Bruges.

Now, twenty-seventeen, we've both quit
and are returning home, you to sit
with friends and me to travel with my wife,
I mention her because I cannot see my life
spent riding you. I draw a really solid dating line
at anyone with bodywork in better shape than mine.

Guy Victory 4856P – Aldridge Transport Museum
The Guy Victory was delivered to Franky Tours in Belgium in 1961. In 1965, there was an accident in the Black Forest, which necessitated a total rebuild. It was repatriated to the UK in April 2017 and was scheduled for restoration.

Not Here

Alison Hallett

You aren't there.

Still, you lie with menace under the sheets. Smirk as I dress. Stand in my way, lazy, entitled, as I move through the house. You sneer when I cook. You follow me into the bathroom, leave barbs in my soap, snare my hair in your hands.

You aren't there.

Still, you block my way. Demand that I skirt round the edges. I tip toe through the house, watching for trip wires. You stand behind me. You walk with one hand on my back and you mock my work. You control my movements and direct my thoughts.

You aren't there.

Still, you stand behind the curtains, stifling your mirth as you cock one foot to trip me up. Scoff when I fall with a smile of concrete and glittering, dangerous eyes. You take a chisel to my shoes. You lie across the sofa. You occupy the air. You sit at the table. You demand respect.

You are not here.

I stop checking the bed for your body. Forget to dread your return. Throw out my heavy armour. I peel off my bandages, slowly, kindly. My tip toeing turns to dancing. I tear down the curtains and jump on the sofa. I waltz from room to room unencumbered; I work without judgement. I cook what I please.

You are not here.

But you reach me. You fire arrows at the house. An envelope on the mat with a trap inside it. Sly words wrapped up in an email. A whisper down the telephone wire to knock me off my feet.

You are still there but not here. Not here.

Escaping

Janet Jenkins

"Taxi! taxi!" shouted Margo
in a busy London street;
she shuffled her feet nervously.
Five black cabs passed by before
she was picked up. "Station please,
as fast as you can. I've no time to waste."

She tried to make plans in her head,
but the driver interrupted her thoughts
with talk of politics, TV and celebs;
she grew more and more fraught
until he took the hint, "I'll leave you
in peace now," he said.

Margo arrived in good time for the train.
She looked back and forth and around
again and again. No sign of HIM.
All seemed safe. "Please God
make it stay that way. I've waited so long."

Time for a coffee maybe; dare I risk it?
No. She spotted him by the entrance.
The one she loathed and feared.
Her sense of foreboding returned. How could
she escape now? How did he know she'd be here?
Could she get through the doors unseen?
Panic set in, nausea, shallow breathing.
He was moving towards her. No. Please no.

"Hello, love!" he shouted,
but HE was a stranger, not her ex.
"Oh sorry, so sorry, I thought you were my wife.
You could be her twin." Margo smiled and took
a deep breath, she couldn't believe the irony.
"No problem at all, I hope you find
my double" and she rushed off to her new life.

Goodbyes and Hellos

Sarah Ann McCay

Rain pounded a repetitive beat on the top of the box as it was slowly lowered into the earth. At a distance, the piper gave a mournful rendition of a marching song.

Maggie clenched the rose in her hand. One of the thorns had punctured her woollen glove and she could feel it biting into her skin. Yet still she couldn't let go.

The rain lashed against her face and mixed with her tears making everything opaque – the people around her merely black and grey blurs. The red of the rose was the only splash of colour to the whole day.

The box was nearly at the six-foot mark. The ropes would soon be loosened. And then the soil would start to rain down on the coffin. But still she clenched at the rose. Its barb stung through the wool, reminding Maggie that she was still alive.

The job now all but done, the funeral director gave her a nod. She froze.

A warm arm reached around her shoulders and a gloved hand took hers, slightly pressing the thorn further into her skin.

For the briefest of moments, Maggie leaned into the body behind her, releasing her tension. The hand squeezed hers softly. Maggie winced as the rose barb dug deeper into her flesh.

Maggie turned.

Sheila smiled.

They hugged. An embrace that made up for nearly a decade of absence.

"I'm sorry," said Sheila.

"So am I," Maggie replied.

Maggie looked up into the face she knew all too well. Her husband's twin, and once her best friend. It was a comfort and a pain to look into the pale blue eyes. A memory stirred – the eyes pleading to be let go but scared of being gone.

The last time they had spoken it had been acrimonious. Sheila had berated Maggie for jumping into a relationship with Sam after his divorce. And there had been a hint of accusation that the main attraction was inheritance. Sam and Sheila's parents had left the twins more than comfortable.

But all Maggie had wanted was to be a part of the family she had more or less grown up with. To feel like she truly belonged. With both Sam and Sheila. Yet somehow that wanting had blown it apart.

"Shall we do this together?" Sheila asked.

Maggie swallowed hard and nodded.

The flower was tangled in the wool of her glove, but between them they worked it free and let it fall.

They watched, holding onto each other, as it landed with the softest of thuds and came to rest on the brass nameplate on the coffin.

Balancing Act

Jayne Stanton

she's no juggler
of feeding bottles, dummies
toddler toys

                                      in her dreams
                              she's a shield maiden,
                        armed with paring knife,
                          potato masher, pan lid

she's had her fill
of breakfast-dinner-tea
plate-spinning

                                      in her dreams
                              she's artful dodger
                                of insults, fists,
                                his bullet points

she's had a mouthful
of pegs to nappies,
those white flags

                                      in her dreams
                                she breathes fire
                                spits razor blades
                        when he cuts her in two

she's done
with walking a tightrope
of washing line

                    she ties her apron
          to the clothes prop, raising her colours
                    like a standard bearer

Shaking Off the Blackness

Janet Jenkins

Black had attached itself to her for months.
She'd tried to remove it, but the sight and sounds
of extreme sickness had made it impossible.
She'd feigned the smile of optimism, offered
reassurance, spoke of the future knowing
her mother had not been fooled.

Black remained after the inevitable day arrived
and although multi colours were worn at the funeral
she couldn't shake it off; the emotional glue
was too strong. Until the walk from the grave
when she spotted something on the path and smiled.
Friends had spoken of robins, crisp packets and feathers
giving signs of the afterlife, she'd always dismissed them

and yet here was a playing card, the Queen of Hearts
sitting in a puddle. Her mum had loved playing whist
and the last time she played there'd been heavy
rain. All nonsense of course, hard to explain,
but bright colours started to reappear and reassure.

SLR

Gary Carr

My camera sits
gun-ugly
on an occasional
table, between us.

Whatever I shoot
is broken-toothed,
unhandsome as decay,
static captured as light.

I sight, square-frame.
Gaze always glassy
behind viewfinders,
ugliest of all.

SLR - Single Lens Reflex (Camera), Self-Loading Rifle (Gun)

Seasons' Entanglement

Alison Sleigh

On cracking thready limbs, winter thundered
across star-pricked horizons
leaving whispering shadows of snowman's dreams.
His following footprints stamped glassy intent
'My path. Mine alone,' he laments.
Shivering with fearful anticipation
scratchy, spindly fingers extended
towards the blossoming grace before him,
beckoning for closeness, while sliding away.
With a final fated flourish of icy lacework
displaying the opulence of his gift to the world
winter shied from spring's radiating passions.
Embarrassed by this desperation
she caressed the frozen heart offering.
Tenderly nuzzling into the coldness,
as cheek stroked cheek,
she contemplated the briefest of unions.
Rituals performed, spring craved summer's touch.

Word of the Day – Entanglement

Marjorie Neilson

Was Jackson ambisinister
or merely clumsy
when he threw paint,
scarring white
canvas with interconnecting,
swirls, drips and splashes
of yellow, blue, and red
in a fury of Abstract
Expressionism?

Or, were his emotions trapped
by the sixties sexual revolution
and iconic femininity of Marilyn
with her swirling white dress
lifted by an updraft
from New York subway grate?
One artist inspiring another.

*Inspired by the painting Entanglement
by Jackson Pollock, and the iconic photograph
of Marilyn Monroe from Some Like it Hot.*

The Fisherman and the Moon

Sarah Dale

Torch guttering at the prow,
weary night nearly over,
dawn fingering eastern sky —
almost time, he thinks,
to turn, take the homing tide

Seeing a silver gleam
starboard he turns, twists, flings
his heavy net up, outwards,
falling sweetly spread,
weighted edge sinking

Deftly, practiced in his art,
he takes the strain, heaving
hand over hand, half amazed
at such weight but reasoning
it's been a long night

Torch is out, but there's no need
for extra light when his whole net
bursts with radiance, spilling
through the mesh; no metaphor
for herring or any other silver fish

When his net brims open on the deck
out steps a moon bright girl,
shining from dripping hair
to high arched dancer's feet;
she looks at him and laughs

What should he do, this lucky fisherman,
but put his coat around her,
take up his oars, row homeward
to his harbour, there being no tide
as he has caught the moon.

The Jasmine Girl and the Fisher's Dream

Mal Dewhirst

Based upon the Irish tale of the wandering Aengus.

Along the stream, the carryin' stream
in the shallows among the reeds,
a trout flips its rainbow gills,
and it pulls against the flow, against
the fisher's line reeling in, reeling in.
He pulls the fish on to the meadow green,
he watches as it twists and writhes,
escaping to skin as a changeling's mask
slips its strings to fall away, fall away.
Her long black hair and pale skin
a crimson dress and ribboned crown,
she plants jasmine in the umber clag earth,
for purity, for luck, for the whispered poetry
then she is gone, she is gone.
The fisher wakes from his dream
he looks in the meadow and along the stream
and searches the night, the stars, the moon,
imagines she's just a wisp away, wisp away.
The jasmine grows along the carryin' stream,
a bride's bouquet of myth and dreams,
sparrows, torment in chattered chant,
as the fisher sits with his line and creel,
waiting for the hushed Jasmine breeze,
her long black hair and pale skin,
dressed in her crimson with ribboned crown,
the fey queen who dances bodhran beat,
marking the pace of his nocturnal trance,
he reaches out to take her hands,
she's only a wisp away, only a wisp away.